# JOURNEY THROUGH
# India

## Anita Ganeri

## Troll Associates

*Library of Congress Cataloging-in-Publication Data*

Ganeri, Anita, (date)
  Journey through India / by Anita Ganeri;
illustrated by Robert Burns ... [et al.].
     p.    cm
  Includes index
  Summary: Describes some of the special
features of such Indian cities as New Delhi,
Calcutta, Madras, and Bombay, as well as
discussing life in the villages and the Hindu
religion.
  ISBN 0-8167-2761-9 (lib. bdg.)
  ISBN 0-8167-2762-7 (pbk.)
  1. India—Description and travel—
1981—Juvenile literature. [1. India]
I. Burns, Robert, ill.   II. Title.
DS414.2.G36   1994
915.404 '52—dc20                91-46176

Published by Troll Associates

© 1994 Eagle Books

Edited by Neil Morris and
Kate Woodhouse
Design by Sally Boothroyd
Picture research by Jan Croot

Illustrators: Robert Burns: 6; Martin
Camm: 4, 5, 19; Chris Forsey: 17; Richard and
Christa Hook: 9, 10, 15; Frank Nichols: 22-23,
24; Ian Thompson: 4-5.

Picture credits: Hutchison Library: 13, 18,
24-25, 25, 30; Hutchison Library/David Chivers:
26, 26-27; Hutchison Library/Carlos Freire: 8,
22, 23; Hutchison Library/Patricio Goycolea: 11,
20; Hutchison Library/M. Harvey: 7;
Hutchison Library/Michael Macintyre: 18-19;
Hutchison Library/Nancy Durrell McKenna:
16; Hutchison Library/Chris Oldroyd: 21;
Hutchison Library/Christine Pemberton: 7, 9;
Hutchison Library/M. Saunders: 28;
Hutchison Library/Nigel Smith: 17; Paul C.
Pet: 16-17; Spectrum: 4-5, 27, 29; Liba Taylor:
25; ZEFA: 1, 10, 12, 13, 14-15, 20-21.

Printed in the U.S.A.
10  9  8  7  6  5  4  3  2  1

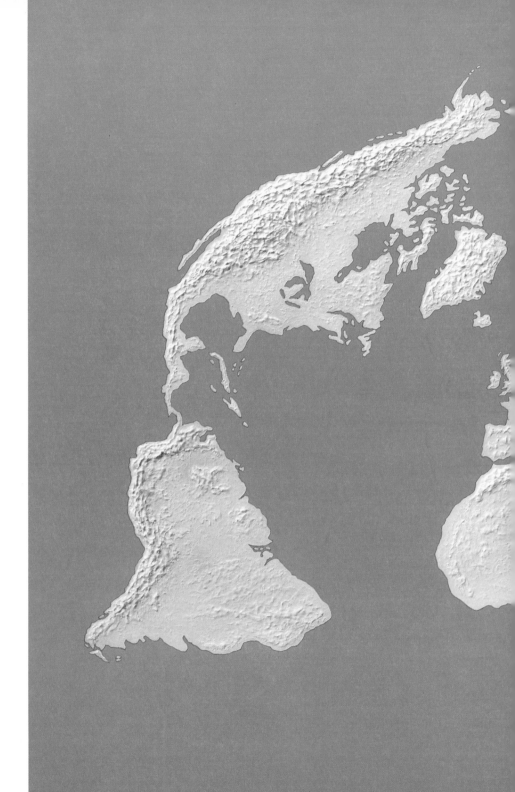

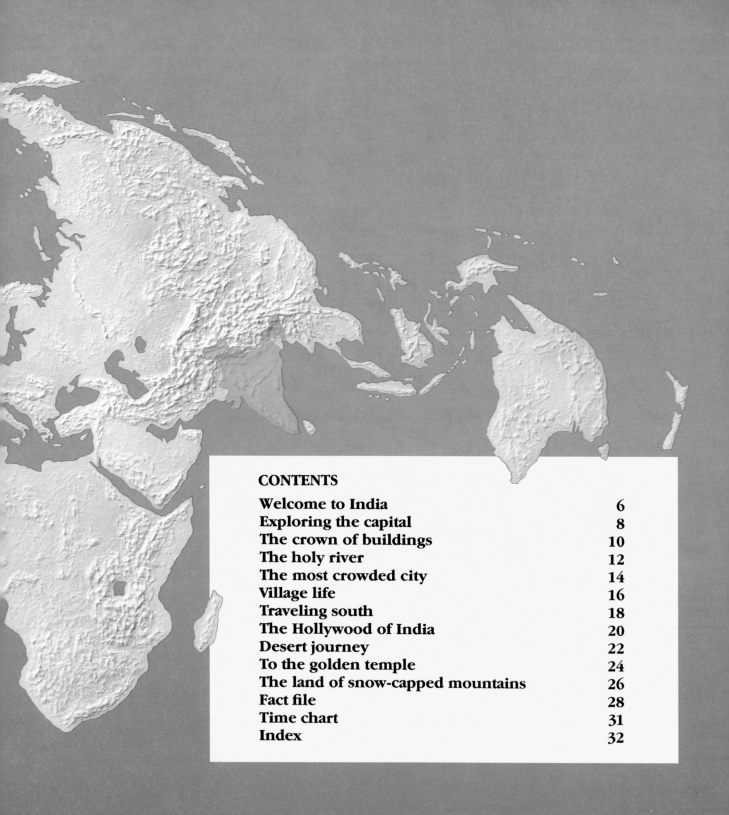

# CONTENTS

# India

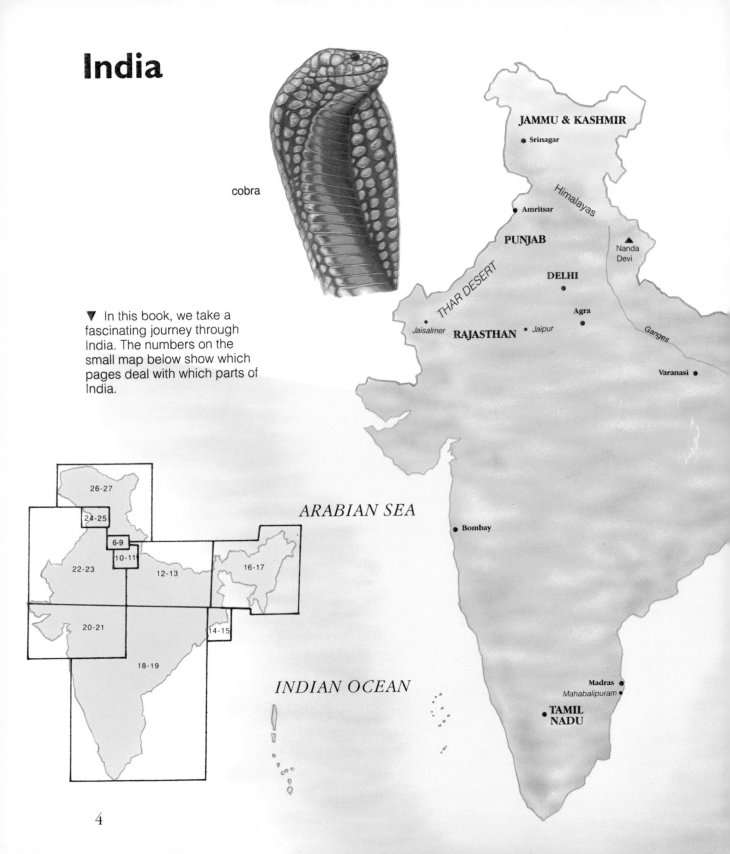

cobra

▼ In this book, we take a fascinating journey through India. The numbers on the small map below show which pages deal with which parts of India.

JAMMU & KASHMIR
• Srinagar

Himalayas

• Amritsar

▲ Nanda Devi

PUNJAB

DELHI •

Agra •

THAR DESERT

Jaisalmer • RAJASTHAN • Jaipur

Ganges

• Varanasi

ARABIAN SEA

• Bombay

INDIAN OCEAN

26-27

24-25

6-9

10-11

22-23

12-13

16-17

20-21

14-15

18-19

Madras •
Mahabalipuram •

TAMIL NADU •

◄ The orange stripe in the Indian flag represents the Hindus and the green stripe the Muslims. The white stripe represents the hope of peace between the two religions. The dark blue wheel is an ancient symbol of the Buddhist religion meaning eternal change.

**Animals of India**
The peacock lives on the plains and is India's national bird. The king cobra is the world's largest poisonous animal. Snake charmers use cobras but remove their harmful fangs.

Brahmaputra

**WEST BENGAL**
• Calcutta

*BAY OF BENGAL*

peacock

**KEY FACTS**

**Area:** 1,269,219 sq. mi. (3,287,263 sq. km.)

**Population:** 833,422,000 – second most populous country after China

**Capital:** New Delhi 5,729,000 people

**Other major cities:** Calcutta 9,194,000 Bombay 8,227,000   Madras 4,289,000

**Highest mountain:** Nanda Devi 25,645 ft. (7,817 m)

**Longest rivers:** Brahmaputra 1,800 mi. (2,896 km.) total   Ganges 1,540 mi. (2,478 km.) total

# Welcome to India

Your first glimpse of India may come as you step off the plane at New Delhi airport. From here you can travel farther by train or in buses covered by flower garlands. There are also rickshaws, boats, two-wheeled ox carts, and even camels to help you explore.

India is a huge country, stretching from mighty snow-capped mountains in the north to palm-fringed beaches in the south. Despite the great distances, Indian people like to travel. They visit their relatives, go to weddings, and make pilgrimages to holy places. The quickest way to travel is by plane, but the most popular way is by train. You can travel in air-conditioned first-class train compartments and sleepers, or on the harder seats of second class.

Wherever you go, you will be given a warm welcome. In north India, people will press the palms of their hands together, bow their heads, and say "*namastey*." This means "hello" in Hindi, India's official language. In the south, people prefer to speak their own language, such as Tamil. But most Indians also speak English, so they can understand each other—and you! Each of India's twenty-five states and seven Union Territories has its own language and there are hundreds of local languages, called dialects. English is widely used in government, business, and higher education.

Each state is like a separate country, with its own people, customs, dress, and food. The people in the south are usually short and dark. They are descended from the earliest Indians, called Dravidians. The taller, fairer northerners are descended from Aryan and Mogul invaders. The British were the last foreigners to control India, ruling the country from 1858 to 1947, when India became independent.

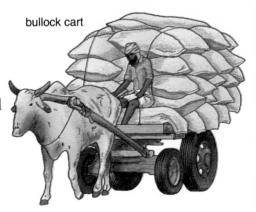

bullock cart

▲ You will see many *sadhus*, or holy men, on your travels.

▲ People in India always seem to be on the move. City streets are packed with cars, trucks, rickshaws, people, and cows. There are about twelve times as many two-wheeled ox carts as cars!

► The most popular form of transportation is the train. India has over 10,000 trains and many are still powered by steam.

# Exploring the capital

From New Delhi airport you can take a taxi or rickshaw into the city itself. If you travel by bus, try to avoid rush hour. The buses are so full that people cling to the sides and even sit on the roof!

New Delhi, the capital city of India, is really two cities – New Delhi and Old Delhi. It is a good starting place for exploring India because the buildings in each part of the city tell many stories from India's long history.

Old Delhi is a walled city with narrow alleyways and bustling bazaars. It was the capital of the Mogul emperors, who ruled India from the 16th to the 19th centuries. They were Muslims and many of the mosques where they worshiped are still standing. The Jama Masjid is the biggest mosque in India. It has room for 25,000 worshipers at a time. At the center of Old Delhi stands the huge Red Fort, and inside you can see rope climbers, magicians, and musicians.

▶ The Jama Masjid is India's largest mosque. It was built from 1644 to 1658 on the orders of the Mogul emperor, Shah Jahan. The mosque has three huge gateways and four towers. It also has two minarets, each standing 131 feet (40 meters) high. They are built of white marble and red sandstone, in vertical stripes.

▼ The Red Fort was also built by Shah Jahan. He started to build it in 1638 on the banks of the Jumna River. The red sandstone walls stretch for 1.5 miles (2.5 kilometers). Within the walls is a fascinating, lively world, which in some ways has not changed for centuries.

▼ The Indian leader, Mahatma Gandhi, was assassinated in Delhi in 1948. A square, black marble platform at Raj Ghat marks the spot where he was cremated.

New Delhi, the official capital, is a modern city with broad streets and high-rise buildings. In 1912, the British, who ruled India at the time, moved the center of government from Calcutta to Delhi. New Delhi was designed and built as the new capital. Rajpath, a huge avenue, runs through the city. At one end stands a great stone arch called India Gate. This was built in memory of Indian soldiers who died in the Second World War. At the other end are government buildings. Today India is one of the biggest democratic republics in the world, with a president, a prime minister, and a parliament.

# The crown of buildings

A luxury air-conditioned bus will take you from Delhi to Agra, to visit one of the most beautiful buildings in the world. The Taj Mahal was built by the Mogul emperor, Shah Jahan, as a tomb for his wife who died in 1629.

From 1526 until the middle of the 19th century India was ruled by the Mogul dynasty. Babur, the first emperor, defeated the sultan of Delhi at the battle of Panipat. He was succeeded by Humayun and then by Akbar, the greatest Mogul emperor, who reigned from 1556 to 1605. Akbar united north India and expanded his empire southward. The Mogul dynasty ruled strongly until the 18th century, when high taxes resulted in peasant revolts, and the empire was divided into a number of regional states whose rulers had little respect for the emperor.

At the same time, the Portuguese, French, Dutch, and English were developing trade links with India. In 1498 Vasco da Gama, a Portuguese explorer, had sailed to India and opened a trade route to Calicut, on the southwest coast. In 1600 the British East India Company was set up as a trading company for tea, cotton, spices, and many other goods.

▲ The Mogul emperor, Shah Jahan, ruled India from 1627 to 1658. He was responsible for many of India's greatest buildings.

◀ The huge Mogul fort at Agra was begun in 1565 by the emperor Akbar. It has an enormous 40 foot (12 meter) thick wall which stretches for 1.5 miles (2.5 kilometers). A moat 33 feet (10 meters) wide runs around the fort. Shah Jahan was deposed and imprisoned in Agra Fort by his son in 1658. He died in a room from which he could see the Taj Mahal.

► The Taj Mahal, which in the Urdu language means "crown of the palace," took over 20 years to build. It was probably designed by a Turkish architect with the help of experts from Persia, France, and Italy. Some 20,000 laborers came from all over India and central Asia to work on this masterpiece. The Taj Mahal is made of white marble, inlaid with semiprecious stones. It stands in the middle of a walled garden, which you reach through a huge red sandstone gateway. Because the Mogul emperors were Muslims, Arabic inscriptions from the Muslim holy book, the Koran, are engraved around the archway. Today about one in ten Indians are Muslims.

Some say the emperor, Shah Jahan, wanted to build a black marble replica of the Taj Mahal for himself on the opposite bank of the Jumna River. He never fulfilled his dream. For the last seven years of his life, the emperor was kept prisoner by his son. He is buried next to his wife in the Taj Mahal.

The Europeans gradually built up their trading links with India, with the British becoming the most powerful influence. In 1784 the India Act gave the British political control of India. During the 19th century the British ruled the country, and in 1876 Queen Victoria was proclaimed empress of India.

# The holy river

Nearly all the main religions of the world are represented in India, but about eight out of ten Indians are Hindus. For them the Ganges, which flows from the Himalayas to the Bay of Bengal, is a holy river. The city of Varanasi, about 15 hours from Delhi by train, lies on the banks of the Ganges. This is the most important holy city of the Hindus. Every year about a million Hindus make a pilgrimage to Varanasi to bathe in the river.

▼ The line of steps running down into the river at Varanasi are called the bathing *ghats*. Pilgrims visit them to take a dip in the holy water of the river. They believe this will cleanse them of their sins. There are also two burning ghats where dead bodies are cremated.

▶ Varanasi is crowded and busy. Fruit and vegetable sellers set up their stalls wherever there is room.

▼ Varanasi is the holiest city for Hindus. There is always a festival or celebration. In September or October, Hindus celebrate *Dussehra*, or *Ramlila*. This is one of the most popular festivals, held in honor of the god, Ram, and his victory over the demon king, Ravana. At the end of the festival people burn huge models of Ravana.

Hindus believe in one supreme being, who is represented by three main gods – Brahma, Vishnu, and Shiva. There are also hundreds of minor gods and goddesses. Hindus worship in temples – there are at least 2,000 temples and shrines in Varanasi alone. They pray to the gods and offer them sweets, fruits, and garlands of flowers. The streets leading to the temples are lined with people selling offerings.

Hindus are divided into four groups, called *castes*. These were originally based on what type of work people did. The highest caste are the Brahmans, many of whom are priests and teachers. Outside the caste system are the Harijans, once considered inferior and untouchable. Many Hindus believe that if they live a good life, they will be born again into a higher caste and a better life.

Varanasi is a lively, noisy place packed with two-wheeled vehicles called tongas and rickshaws. Cows wander the streets, holding up the traffic and stealing vegetables from wayside stalls, but they are never harmed because they are considered sacred animals.

# The most crowded city

Arriving in Calcutta is an adventure in itself. The train from Varanasi drops you at Howrah station. Here there is constant hustle and bustle. People crowd the platforms to board trains or sell anything from fruit to new sandals. A porter will hoist your luggage onto his head and take you outside to catch a taxi or rickshaw across the bridge into the city.

Calcutta is the largest city in India, with over nine million residents. Many of its people are very poor. Some are refugees from Bangladesh, which was part of Pakistan until 1971. Others are villagers who have come to the city to look for work. Many end up begging and even sleeping on the streets. In contrast, Calcutta has many rich business people who live in comfortable apartments.

In India's big cities, children from poor families often work during the day and go to school in the evening. Indian children are entitled to free education from the ages of six to twelve. Many then leave to go out to work. If their parents are better off financially, children may stay in school and continue their studies.

Calcutta is the capital of the state of West Bengal. It is famous for its artists and poets, and has one university and several colleges. There is plenty to do for children living in the city, including trips to the botanical gardens, the zoo, the museum, or the planetarium. In the center of the city is a huge park where people play cricket, hockey, soccer, and fly kites. Here you may also see people discussing politics or doing their yoga exercises.

▶ Calcutta is one of the world's most crowded cities. During the rush hour, traffic chokes the streets. Cars, trams, people, and stray cows seem to be everywhere. There is a deafening sound of honking car horns.

▶ Most Indians are cricket mad. They will play whenever they can, even if they have to share a set of pads! The famous cricket ground in Calcutta is called Eden Gardens. During the five days of a test match every seat in the stadium is full. Outside the stadium, people play cricket, watch it on television, listen to the match commentary on the radio, and discuss the performance of the national team. Many people even take their vacation at this time.

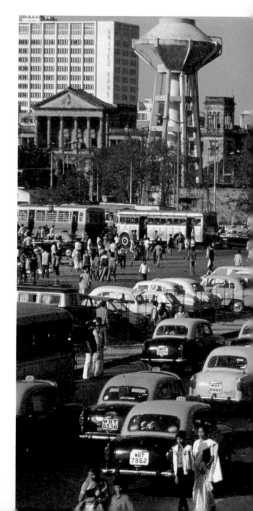

▼ Mother Theresa became famous throughout the world for her work among the lepers and homeless people of Calcutta.

# Village life

A short bus ride will take you out of Calcutta and into the countryside. Here life is very different. Four out of five Indians live in villages, and there are half a million villages in India! Most villagers work as farmers, growing rice, wheat, sugar cane, lentils, and chickpeas. The work is hard and most farmers are quite poor.

The village day starts early, before it gets too hot. The men and boys set off for the fields to tend their crops. Many farmers still use two-wheeled ox carts to pull their plows, and they harvest their crops by hand. Water is scarce in India, and the farmers rely heavily on the torrential monsoon rains that fall in summer. If the rains fail, the whole crop is lost. But if the rains are too heavy the fields may flood.

◄ In some parts of India, villagers work on tea plantations. India is the greatest producer of tea in the world. The tea is picked by hand – it is hard work!

▼ Very few village farmers can afford modern machinery such as tractors or plows. Most farmers still use wooden plows pulled along by bullocks.

◄ Some villages have a school run by a teacher or village elder. The children sit outdoors, on the ground, and study their lessons.

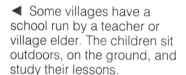

Village women and girls prepare the day's food and do the housework. Fresh vegetables and spices bought at the market are eaten with rice or *chapatis*, a type of flat bread. People eat with their fingers off metal plates or banana leaves. There is water or sweet, milky tea to drink. Food is often cooked outdoors over a fire.

Twice a day, girls fetch water from the well, the most important place in the village.

The day ends with a family meal around the fire, sometimes followed by a story.

Then it is early to bed!

# Traveling south

If you decide to travel south by train, make sure you book a comfortable seat. The journey from Calcutta to Madras takes 25 hours. If you are in a hurry, you can fly in just two hours.

As you travel south, the people, scenery, and climate all change. Southern India is hotter than the north. Palm trees fringe the roadside and rice, India's main crop, is grown in flooded paddy fields. The food in south India, curries and spicy vegetarian dishes, is much hotter, too.

▲ The shore temples at Mahabalipuram are well worth a visit. These simple but very beautiful shrines date from the 7th century. They are devoted to the Hindu gods Shiva and Vishnu.

◄ South India is famous for its dancers. The most colorful style of dance, called *Kathakali*, was first performed some 2,000 years ago. Only men can dance the lead roles. They wear elaborate masks or make-up and stunning costumes. The dances tell stories of gods and demons.

Madras is the capital of the southern state of Tamil Nadu. It is the fourth largest city in India, but the pace of life is slower than in the northern cities. You can take a city bus tour and visit the museum, the English fort, or the snake park. Then you could have a refreshing drink of coconut milk from a roadside stall.

Most people in south India are Hindus. Everywhere you go you will see temples with high towers covered in carvings. These are the temple gateways. They lead into a bustling temple town with courtyards and huge, pillared halls. Stalls sell garlands and offerings for the gods, as well as pictures of the gods and holy men to take away as souvenirs.

▲ Indian tigers are very rare and closely protected. You might be lucky and see one at the Periyar Wildlife Sanctuary in Tamil Nadu.

# The Hollywood of India

When the British ruled the country, Bombay was called the "gateway to India." Huge passenger ships docked in Bombay's port, bringing thousands of new arrivals. Bombay is still the busiest port in India, but most people now arrive in the city by plane or train.

Today this lively, bustling city has another nickname. It is known as the "Hollywood of India" and is the center of India's thriving film industry, the largest in the world. Over 600 full-length films are made in India every year, nearly half of them in Bombay. The films are action-packed mixtures of song, dance, daring adventure, and romance. Many film stars live in Bombay. They are great heroes and often go on to become politicians. Indians love going to the movies. An amazing nine million tickets are sold every day, more than anywhere else in the world. Don't miss joining the filmgoers if you are in Bombay!

Bombay is one of the main centers of industry in India. Factories make cars, chemicals, bicycles, and textiles. It is also India's most modern city, with high-rise office buildings and skyscrapers. Each day tens of thousands of office workers arrive by train to work in the city. At 12 o'clock the workers receive their lunchboxes. Each of these packed lunches is cooked at home, picked up at special points, and taken by train to the city. Astonishingly, each one is delivered to the right person on time every day.

▲ Bombay has a large, very modern harbor and port. It is set against a backdrop of skyscrapers, office buildings, and hotels. Further along the sea front, you may see small, wooden, traditional fishing boats setting out to sea. Women sell the catch at the docks.

▶ The Gateway of India overlooks Bombay harbor. It was built in 1925 to commemorate a visit by George V.

◀ You will see huge, brightly-colored posters all over Bombay. These advertise the latest films. You won't be able to miss the movie theaters – or the long lines of people!

# Desert journey

The quickest way to get from Bombay to the northwestern state of Rajasthan is to fly. But for a more exciting journey you could go back to Delhi and catch a special train called the "Palace on Wheels." The carriages that make up this train all used to belong to *maharajas*, or Indian princes.

Rajasthan is a land of princes, palaces, and desert. Hundreds of years ago it was the home of Rajput warriors who built great forts high up on the hillsides. When the British ruled India, Rajasthan was split into separate states governed by princes. Jaipur, the capital of Rajasthan, still has its own maharaja, who lives in the City Palace.

▶ The Hava Mahal, or Wind Palace, is one of Jaipur's most famous landmarks. It stands on the main street of the old city. The five-story building is just a facade, designed so that the wind could cool it down naturally. This is how it was so named. It was built by Maharaja Sawaj Pratap Singh. Climb to the top for a wonderful view of the city.

▲ Camels are the most common form of transportation in Rajasthan. Each year in November, a huge fair is held in the city of Pushkar. Camel racing is one of the most popular sights there.

▶ Trains have always been a popular means of transportation, even for the richest people of India. The "Palace on Wheels" is just what you would expect from its name.

Jaipur is called the "pink city" because it has many sandstone buildings which glow pink in the evening sun. On the main street you can see the famous Hava Mahal, or Wind Palace. This is a sandstone screen with carved balconies and windows. It was built in 1799 for the ladies of the royal court. They would sit behind the screen and watch life in the street below, without being seen themselves. Camel carts are a common sight in the streets of Jaipur, as well as rickshaws and bicycles. As you go farther west towards the Thar Desert, everyone travels by camel, even letter carriers.

In the city of Jaisalmer you can hire a camel for a trek into the desert. Don't forget to take plenty of water, something to cover your head, and a cushion!

# To the golden temple

To the north of Rajasthan lies the state of Punjab. This is the wealthiest state in India, producing more wheat and rice than anywhere else. The name *Punjab* means "five rivers." These rivers provide plenty of water for growing crops.

Most people in Punjab are Sikhs. They follow a religion begun about 500 years ago by a holy man, Guru Nanak. All Sikh men have the surname Singh, which means "lion." Sikhs of previous generations were given this name because they had to be good fighters to protect themselves from people of other religions. Sikh men also have five symbols of their faith, the so-called five Ks: *kesh* (uncut hair), *kara* (steel bracelet), *kangha* (wooden comb), *kacchha* (shorts), and *kirpan* (sword). These were introduced so that Sikhs could recognize each other easily.

The city of Amritsar is the Sikhs' holiest city. Thousands of pilgrims come here every year to visit the Golden Temple. This Sikh shrine stands in a sacred pool with beautiful gardens nearby. You must take off your shoes and cover your head before you enter the temple.

Today the Golden Temple has become the symbol of the struggle between some Sikhs and the Indian government. The Sikhs want Punjab to become a separate country called Khalistan. This has led to violence and unrest. In 1984 India's prime minister, Indira Gandhi, was assassinated by two of her Sikh bodyguards after the occupation of the Golden Temple by Indian troops.

► The Sikhs' holy book is the *Granth Sahib*. The original copy is kept inside the Golden Temple. Every day, a priest sits and reads from the holy writings. His voice is broadcast to worshipers outside the temple.

kirpan

► Today there are about 15 million Sikhs in India. The men are easy to recognize because of their turbans and long beards.

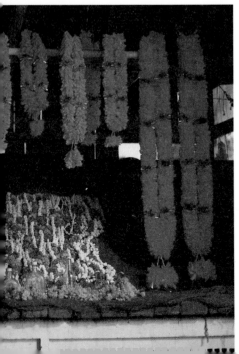

▲ Chandigarh is the capital of the Punjab. It is a very modern city, built in the 1950s and designed by the French architect Le Corbusier.

25

# The land of snow-capped mountains

The last stage of our journey takes us to the far north and Kashmir, where snow-capped mountains rise high into the sky. These are part of the mighty Himalayas, which stretch for 1,500 miles (2,400 kilometers) across India. All the major rivers of India spring from glaciers in the Himalayas. You may want to fly to Srinagar, the capital of the state of "Jammu and Kashmir." Most Kashmiris are Muslims, and parts of the region of Kashmir are controlled by Pakistan and China. Kashmir has frequently been fought over by India and Pakistan.

The Mogul emperors used to come to Srinagar in the summer to escape from the heat farther south. You can visit the grand gardens they designed. Srinagar stands on the Dal Lake, where visitors can stay in houseboats at the water's edge. You can explore the lake in a long, narrow boat called a *shikara* and buy fruit, vegetables, and snacks from other shikaras as they float by. Then stop on Silver or Gold Island and have a picnic.

Kashmir is famous for its carpets, papier mâché boxes, and shawls. *Cashmere* wool comes from the goats of Kashmir. If you stroll around the markets in the evening, you will notice people dressed in long, flowing robes to keep warm. Don't worry if they have a strange shape. Under their robes they are carrying little clay pots filled with hot coals for extra warmth.

Our journey through India has taken us from modern cities, sacred buildings, simple villages, and barren deserts, to the beautiful snow-capped north. But no matter where you go, India is a fascinating country you will never forget.

► If you are feeling energetic, you could go trekking in the mountains of Kashmir.

◄ Each year, thousands of Hindu pilgrims make the long journey from Phalagam outside Srinagar to the sacred Amarnath Cave, high up in the mountains. The cave is a shrine to the god, Shiva.

▼ *Shikaras* on the Dal Lake are used for transportation and as market stalls. People buy, sell, and barter from their boats. The lake is a very busy place. There is always something happening.

# Fact file

## The languages of India

India has 15 main languages, over 200 minor languages, and about 1,000 local dialects. The official national language is Hindi, which is the native language of almost 30 percent of people. Other major languages include Telugu, Bengali, Marathi, Tamil, and Urdu.

Indian languages use different alphabets. Hindi is written in the Devanagri alphabet. The letters in each word are linked with a line running across the top. Tamil is based on the ancient languages of the Dravidians, the earliest people to live in India. Urdu, spoken by many Muslims, is written in the Arabic script.

## Borders

India is shaped something like a triangle. The Himalaya mountains mark India's northern borders with Nepal, China, and Bhutan. To the northwest, India borders Pakistan, and to the northeast, Bangladesh. Before India became an independent country in 1947, these borders did not exist. Pakistan and Bangladesh were part of India.

## Coastline

India's coastline stretches for about 3,500 miles (5,600 kilometers). Off the west coast is the Arabian Sea and off the east coast, the Bay of Bengal. These bodies of water join the Indian Ocean to the south. The Andaman and Nicobar Islands in the Bay of Bengal and the Lakshadweep Islands in the Arabian Sea are Union Territories and part of India. The island of Sri Lanka to the south is a separate country.

| Hindi | English | | Hindi | English |
|---|---|---|---|---|
| नमस्ते | hello — HINDI | | | |
| आप कैसे हैं ? | How are you? | | | |
| हाँ | yes | | | |
| नहीं | no | | | |
| एक | 1 | | छह | 6 |
| दो | 2 | | सात | 7 |
| तीन | 3 | | आठ | 8 |
| चार | 4 | | नौ | 9 |
| पांच | 5 | | दस | 10 |

◄ This is a *stupa*, a holy shrine of Buddhism. Stupas are believed to hold relics and possessions of the Buddha.

## Population

One out of every six people in the world is Indian. About 30,000 babies are born every day in India. By the year 2,000 India's population may reach one billion. It would be very difficult to feed this amount of people, and the Indian government is now encouraging people to have smaller families.

## Indian religions

**Hinduism** About eight out of ten Indians are Hindus. The Hindu religion is ancient, dating back about 5,000 years. Hindus believe in one supreme being called Brahman. He is represented by three main gods: Brahma, the creator of the universe; Vishnu, the preserver; and Shiva, the destroyer. Hindus believe if they live good lives they will be reborn into a higher caste.

**Islam** About one Indian in ten is Muslim and follows the religion of Islam. They believe in one god, Allah, who revealed his teachings to the prophet Mohammed. The Muslim holy book is called the Koran.

**Buddhism** The Buddhist religion was founded some 2,500 years ago by an Indian prince, Siddhartha Gautama. He became known as the Buddha. Today there are about five million Buddhists in India and many more in Japan, China, and Thailand.

**Sikhism** A holy man, Guru Nanak, founded the Sikh religion about 500 years ago. Sikhs worship in temples called *gurdwaras*. Their holy book is called the Granth Sahib. There are about 15 million Sikhs in India.

**Other religions** About three and a half million Indians are Jains, an ancient Hindu sect. About 120,000 are Zoroastrians, who worship a fire god called Ahura Mazda. There is also a small percentage of Christians and Jews in India.

▶ A mouth-watering display of snacks outside the Amber Fort in Rajasthan. You can pick whatever you like from this brightly colored display.

## The Hindu calendar

In their daily lives, Indians use the same calendar as we do. For religious purposes Hindus use a special calendar based on the phases of the moon. Each month runs from full moon to full moon and is split into a light half and a dark half. Below you can see the seasons and months of the Hindu calendar.

| Season | Hindu month | English month |
|---|---|---|
| Vasanta | Chait | March-April |
| (Spring) | Baisakh | April-May |
| Grishma | Jeth | May-June |
| (Summer) | Ashab | June-July |
| Varsha | Sawan | July-August |
| (Rainy) | Bhadon | August-September |
| Sharada | Asvin | September-October |
| (Autumn) | Kartik | October-November |
| Hemanta | Aghan | November-December |
| (Winter) | Pushya | December-January |
| Shishira | Magha | January-February |
| (Dewy) | Phalgun | February-March |

The calendar is also divided into *eras*, or long periods of time. The two most important are the Vikrama era, which began in 58 B.C., and the Shaka era, which began in A.D. 78.

## Railways

India has the fourth largest railway system in the world. It has nearly 38,000 miles (60,000 kilometers) of track and about 11,000 locomotives. It is thought that 10 million people travel by train each day.

▲ These huge and intricate figures in the caves of Ellora, northwest of Bombay, were carved out of solid rock hundreds of years ago.

## Hindu horoscopes

When most Hindu babies are born, priests draw up a horoscope. The horoscope begins with a prayer to the gods and ends with a blessing. It shows the positions of the sun, moon, and stars at the time of the baby's birth and its sign of the zodiac. Horoscopes are written in *Sanskrit*, an ancient Indian language.

## Farming and industry

Nearly three-quarters of Indians work on the land. The main food crops are rice, wheat, lentils, and chickpeas. India is the world's top producer of tea. About 750,000 tons (682,500 metric tons) of tea are grown every year, especially in Assam and Darjeeling.

India is one of the world's top twelve industrial nations. It produces huge amounts of iron, steel, and textiles, such as cotton, silk, and jute, a fiber used to make sacks and cord.

| B.C. | Time chart |
|---|---|
| c3000 | Farming villages begin in the Indus river valley. |
| c2500 | Beginning of an advanced Indus civilization, with the great cities of Mahenjo Daro and Harappa. |
| c1500 | Aryans invade India from the north and spread through the country. |
| c150-500 | Hindu religion established. Vedas (holy books) composed and caste system developed. |
| c563 | Siddhartha Gautama, the Buddha, is born. His ideas form the Buddhist religion. |
| c170 | Greeks invade northwest India and set up Greek states in the Punjab. |
| **A.D.** | |
| 50 | North India invaded by Kushans and nomads from Bactria. |
| 195-405 | Parthians from central Asia rule north India. |
| 320 | Gupta Empire founded by Chandragupta. The Hindu religion revives. |
| 535 | Huns invade from central Asia. India splits up into warring Hindu kingdoms. |
| 1192 | Arabs invade north India. |
| 1206 | The reign of the Islamic Sultanate of Delhi begins, expanding Arab rule. |
| 1336 | The Hindu empire of Vijayanagar rebels against Arab rule. |
| 1498 | The explorer, Vasco da Gama, sails to India, opening up a trade route for the Portuguese. |
| 1526 | Babur defeats the Sultan of Delhi at the Battle of Panipat and establishes the Mogul Empire. |
| 1556-1605 | Reign of Akbar, the greatest Mogul emperor. He unites north India and expands southward. |
| 1611 | The British East India Company sets up a trading base at Surat. |
| 1632 | Shah Jahan begins building the Taj Mahal. |
| 1784 | The India Act. The British take political control of India. |
| 1857 | The First War of Independence (Indian Mutiny). Bengali troops rise against the British. |
| 1858 | British government appoints a viceroy to rule India. Start of the British *Raj* (rule). |
| 1876 | Queen Victoria proclaimed empress of India. |
| 1885 | Indian National Congress founded the first national political party. |
| 1919 | Amritsar massacre. A large number of Indians were killed by British troops. |
| 1920 | Mohandas (Mahatma) Gandhi begins campaign of nonviolent civil disobedience against British rule. Unrest throughout India. |
| 1947 | India gains independence. Jawaharlal Nehru becomes its first prime minister. Pakistan made separate country. Civil war in Kashmir. |
| 1950 | India becomes a democratic republic within the Commonwealth of Nations. |
| 1966 | Indira Gandhi, Nehru's daughter, becomes prime minister of India. |
| 1971 | India is at war with Pakistan. East Pakistan becomes the independent country of Bangladesh. |
| 1984 | Sikhs call for an independent Punjab. Indira Gandhi is assassinated. Her son, Rajiv, becomes prime minister. |
| 1989 | Rajiv Gandhi and the Congress Party are defeated and the Janata (people's) Party are elected. |
| 1991 | Rajiv Gandhi assassinated during election campaign. |

# Index